SIMPLE CHRISTMAS SONGS
FOR GUITAR

ISBN 978-1-4950-9723-2

HAL•LEONARD®

7777 W. BLUEMOUND RD. P.O. BOX 13819 MILWAUKEE, WI 53213

Visit Hal Leonard Online at
www.halleonard.com

All I Want for Christmas Is My Two Front Teeth

Words and Music by Don Gardner

D   G   E7   A7   G#°7   F#7   Bm

Key of D
Chorus
Moderately

D / **E7** / **A7**
4/4 All I want for Christmas is my | two front teeth, my | two front teeth, see my |

D / **E7**
two front teeth. | Gee, if I could only have my | two front teeth, then |

A7 / **D** / **Verse** / **G**
I could wish you, "Merry | Christmas!" | 1. It ‖: seems so long since
2. *Spoken:* | *Good ol' Santa Claus and* |

G#°7 / **D** / **A7** / **D** / **F#7**
I could say, | "Sister Suzy sitting on a | thistle." |
all his reindeer they | *used to bring me lots of toys and* | *candy.* *Gee, but* |

Bm
Ev'ry time I | try to speak, |
now when I go out and call, | *"Dancer, Prancer, Donner and Blitzen,"* |

E7 / **A7** / **N.C.**
all I do is | whistle. ⎫
none of them can understand | *me.* ⎭ *Whistled: Ss!* ‖

Outro-Chorus

D / **E7** / **A7**
All I want for Christmas is my | two front teeth, my | two front teeth, see my |

D / **E7**
two front teeth. | Gee, if I could only have my |

1.

G **G#°7** / **D** / **A7** / **D** **N.C.**
two front teeth, then | I could wish you, "Merry | Christmas!" :‖

2.

D / **N.C.**
Christmas!" | Christ - | mas. Christmas. *Oh,* |

D
for goodness sakes! | *Happy New Year!* | ‖

Blue Christmas

Words and Music by Billy Hayes and Jay Johnson

E   B7   E7   A   F#7   A#°7

231   213 4   2 1   123   321   12 3

Key of E

Moderately (♪♪ = ♪♪³)

% Verse

E
4/4 1. I'll have a   ‖: blue   Christmas   with - out you.
               blue   snowflakes   start | fall - in',
               (3.) Instrumental

I'll be so | blue   just | thinking   a -
that's when so those | blue | mem'ries   start

E
bout you.   Dec - o - ra   tions of
call - in'   *Instrumental ends* ⎱| (2., 3.) You'll be | do   in' all

1.

E7
red   on a | green Christmas | tree
right with your

F#7   B7   N.C.
won't be the | same, dear,   if | you're not here with | me. 2. And when the :‖

2.

A   A#°7   B7
Christmas   of | white, but | I'll have a | blue,   blue, blue, blue

To Coda ⊕   *D.S. al Coda*   ⊕ *Coda*
                               (take 2nd ending)

E
Christmas.   N.C.
                   | 3. Instrumental   ‖ | ‖

All I Want for Christmas Is You

Words and Music by Mariah Carey and Walter Afanasieff

G   G/B   C   D7   Cm   B7   Em   E7   Am7

Key of G
Intro
Freely

G
$\frac{4}{4}$ I don't want a lot   for Christmas; | there is just one thing   I need. |

C   **Cm**
| I don't care about   the presents | underneath   the Christ | - mas tree. |

G   **B7**   **Em**   **Cm**
| I just want you for | my own, | more than you could ev | - er know. |

G   **E7**   **Am7**   **D7**
| Make my wish come true. | All I want for | Christmas is |

Moderately fast (♫ = ♩♪)

G   **Em**   **Am7**   **D7**
| you. | | | ‖

Verse

G
‖: 1. I don't want a lot | for Christmas; | there is just one thing | I need. And I |
2. I won't ask for much | this Christmas; | I won't e - ven wish | for snow. And I,

C   **Cm**
| don't care about | the pres - ents | underneath the Christ | - mas tree. |
| I'm just gonna | keep on wait - ing | underneath the mis | - tle - toe. |

G
| I don't need to hang | my stock-ing | there up - on the fi | re - place. |
| I won't make a list | and send it | to the North Pole for | Saint Nick. |

C   **Cm**
| Santa Claus won't make | me hap - py | with a toy on Christ | - mas Day. |
| I won't e - ven stay | a - wake to | hear those mag - ic rein | - deer click. 'Cause |

G   **B7**   **Em**   **Cm**
| I just want you for | my own, | more than you could ev | - er know. |
| I just want you here | to - night, | holding on to me so | tight. |

G		**E7**	**Am7**		**D7**	
Make my wish come true.			All I want for	Christmas is		
What more can I do?						

1. / 2.

G	**Em**	**Am7**	**D7**	**D7**	
you,		you,	baby, oh. :‖	baby, oh. ‖	

Bridge

B7			**Em**	
All the lights	are shining so	brightly ev'rywhere,		

B7			**Em**	
and the sound	of children's	laughter fills the air.		

Cm		**G**	**E7**	
And ev'ryone	is singing,	I hear those sleigh	bells ringing.	

Am7		**D7**		
Santa, won't you please bring me	what I really need? Won't you	please bring my baby to me?	Oh, ‖	

Outro-Verse

G				
I don't want a lot	for Christmas,	this is all I'm	asking for:	

C		**Cm**		
I just want to see	my baby	standing right outside	my door.	

G	**B7**	**Em**		**Cm**
I just want you for	my own,	more than you could ev	- er know.	

G	**E7**	**Am7**	**Cm**	
Make my wish come true:	Baby,	all I want for	Christmas	

	G	**Em**	**Am7**	**D7**
is	you.		Ooh,	baby. ‖

Repeat and fade

G	**Em**	**Am7**	**D7**
‖: All I want for	Christmas is	you,	baby. :‖

5

Baby, It's Cold Outside

from the Motion Picture NEPTUNE'S DAUGHTER

By Frank Loesser

D   Em7   A7   D7   G   G7   E7   Dm6   B7

Key of D

Moderately

Verse

D

1. *Female:* I really can't stay,   I've got to go 'way.
Male: But, baby, it's cold outside.   But, baby, it's cold
simply must go,   the an-swer is, "No!"
2. *Male:* But, baby, it's cold outside.   But, baby, it's cold

Em7

Em7   **A7**   **A7**

D

outside.   This evening has been   so very
Been hoping that you'd drop in.
outside.   This welcome has been   so nice and
How lucky that you dropped in.

D7

nice.   My mother will start to
I'll hold your hands, they're just like ice.
warm.   My sister will be sus -
Look out the win - dow at that storm.

G

G7

wor - ry   and father will be pacing the floor.   So
Beau - ti - ful, what's your hurry?   Lis - ten to the fireplace
pi - cious, my brother will be there at the door.   My
Gosh, your lips look de - licious.   Waves up - on a tropical

D

E7

really I'd better scur - ry,   well, maybe just a half a drink
roar.   Beau - ti - ful, please don't hurry.
maiden aunt's mind is vi - cious,   well, maybe just a cig - a - rette
shore.   Ooh, your lips are de - licious.

| **A7**   **D**
more.   The neigh-bors might think,   hey,
| Put some rec-ords on while I pour.   But, baby, it's bad | out   there.
| more.   I've | got to get home,   say, |
| Nev - er such a bliz-zard be - fore.   But baby, you'd freeze out   there.

Em7   **A7**   **Em7**   **A7**   **D**
what's in this drink?   I   wish I knew how
| lend me a comb.   No cabs to be had | out there.   Your eyes are like star- |
| It's up to your knees out there. You've| real-ly been grand
| I   thrill when you touch

                              D7
| to   break the   spell.   I
| - light   now.   I'll   take your hat, | your hair looks   There's |
| but   don't you | see?   How   can   you do   this thing to
| my hand.   light now.

G   **D**   **Dm6**   **E7**
ought to say, "No, no,   no, sir!"   At   least I'm gon - na say that I
| swell. | Mind if I   move   in | clos - er?   At   least there will be plen - ty im - |
| bound to be talk to - | mor - row,   at | least there will be plen - ty im - |
| me?   Think of my   life - long   sor - row

A7   **D**
tried.   I   really   can't   stay,
| What's the sense   of hurt - ing my pride? | really   can't   stay,   Oh, baby,   don't hold |
| plied.   I   really   can't   stay,
| if you caught pneu - mo - nia and died. Get   over   that old

B7   **E7**   **A7**
                    ah,   but   it's   cold   out   -
| out,   ba - by,   it's   cold | out   - |
| ah,   but   it's   cold   out   -
| doubt,   ba - by,   it's   cold   out   -

|1. ||2.
D   **A7**   **D**   **A7**   **D**
| side. | 2. *Female:* I   :|| side ||
| side.   side.

Believe

from Warner Bros. Pictures' THE POLAR EXPRESS

Words and Music by Glen Ballard and Alan Silvestri

C   Em   Dm7   B7   Fmaj7   G   B♭   Gsus4   E7#5   Am

Key of C
Verse
Moderately slow

C
4/4 1. Chil - dren | sleeping, | snow is softly
2. Trains move | quickly | to their journey's

Em ... **C**

Em
falling. | Dreams are | calling
end. | Des - ti - | nations

Dm7 ... **B7**

Dm7
like bells in the | dis - tance. | We were
are where we be -| gin again. | Ships go

Fmaj7 **G** **C**

Em **C** **Em** **Dm**
dreamers, | not so long ago, | | but one by
sailing | far a - cross the sea, | | trust - ing

B7 **Dm7** **Fmaj7** **G**
one, we | all had to | grow up.
star - light | to get where they | need to be.

Pre-Chorus

Em **F**
When it seems the magic slipped a - | way, we
When it seemed that we have lost our | way, we

B♭ **Gsus4** **G**
find it all again on Christmas | Day. } Be -
find our - selves again on Christmas | Day. }

Chorus

C			Dm7		C		Fmaj7	
lieve	in	what your heart is saying,	hear	the mel - o - dy that's playing				

C	G	Dm7	G	C	Dm7
There's no time to waste, there's so	much to cel - e - brate.	Be -	lieve in what you feel inside	and	

C	E7♯5	Am	Dm7
give your dreams the wings to	fly.	You have ev'rything you	need

Gsus4	C	_1._	Em	_2._ C	
if you just	believe.			:‖ believe.	

Outro

Fmaj7	C	G	Dm7 Gsus4	C	Dm7
If you just	believe,		if you just	believe,	

C	F	C	G	Dm7 Gsus4	C	Dm7
if you just	believe.		Just	be - lieve,		

C	F	C	G	Dm7	Gsus4
just	believe.				

Repeat and fade

‖: | C | Dm7 | C | F | C | G | Dm7 | Gsus4 | :‖

Caroling, Caroling

Words by Wihla Hutson
Music by Alfred Burt

G Bm Am D7 Em Bm7 E9 A7 D C

Key of G
Verse
Moderately fast

G	Bm		G		Bm	Am	D7	
1. Caroling,	caroling,		now	we	go;	Christmas	bells	are
2. Caroling,	caroling,		through	the	town;	Christmas	bells	are
3. Caroling,	caroling,		near	and	far;	Christmas	bells	are

G	Em		Bm7	E9		Bm7		E9
ring	- ing!		Caroling,	caroling,		through	the	snow;
ring	- ing!		Caroling,	caroling,		up	and	down;
ring	- ing!		Following,	following,		yon	- der	star;

Em	A7		D			Am		
Christmas	bells	are	ring	- ing!		Joy	- ous voic	- es
Christmas	bells	are	ring	- ing!		Mark	ye	well	the
Christmas	bells	are	ring	- ing!		Sing	we	all	this

D				G			Em	
sweet	and	clear,		sing	the	sad	of	heart	to cheer.
song	we	sing,		glad	- some	tid	- ings	now	we bring.
hap	- py	morn,		"Lo,	the	King	of	heav'n	is born!"

C	G		D7	G		Am		D7
Ding	dong,		ding,	dong,		Christmas	bells	are

1., 2.				3.			
G				**G**			
ring	-	ing!		ring	-	ing!	

A Child Is Born

Music by Thad Jones
Lyrics by Alec Wilder

Cmaj7   Fm6   Fmaj7♭5   E7   Am7   D7   Dm7   G7   E7♯5   Fmaj7   B♭9

Key of C
Verse
Slow

Cmaj7			Fm6			Cmaj7			Fm6		
¾ Now			out	of	the	night,			new	as	the

Cmaj7			Fm6			Fmaj7♭5			E7		
dawn,			into		the	light,			this		

Am7			E7			Am7			E7		
child,			innocent			child,			soft	as	a

Am7			D7			Dm7			G7		
fawn,			this	child	is	born.			One		small

Outro-Verse

Cmaj7			Fm6			Cmaj7			Fm6		
heart,			one	pair	of	eyes,			one	work	of

Cmaj7			E7♯5			Fmaj7			B♭9		
art			here	in	my	arms,			here		He

Cmaj7			Fm6			Am7			D7		
lies			trusting	and	warm,			blessed		this

Dm7			G7			Cmaj7			Fm6		
morn,		a	child	is	born.					

Cmaj7			Fm6			Cmaj7		

The Chipmunk Song

Words and Music by Ross Bagdasarian

G   D7   Am7   G7   C   Cm   A7

Key of G
Verse
Moderately fast

G			**D7**		
3/4 Christmas,		Christmas	time	is	near,

			G		
time	for	toys	and	time	for	cheer.

Am7		**D7**		**Am7**		**D7**	
We've	been	good,	but	we	can't	last.

Am7		**D7**		**G**	
Hurry,		Christmas,		hurry	fast!

Want	a	plane	that	loops	the	loop.

		G7		**C**	
Me,	I	want	a	Hula	-	Hoop.

		Cm		**G**		**A7**	
We	can	hardly	stand	the	wait.	Please

Am7		**D7**		**G**	
Chistmas,		don't	be	late!

The Christmas Song
(Chestnuts Roasting on an Open Fire)

Music and Lyric by Mel Torme and Robert Wells

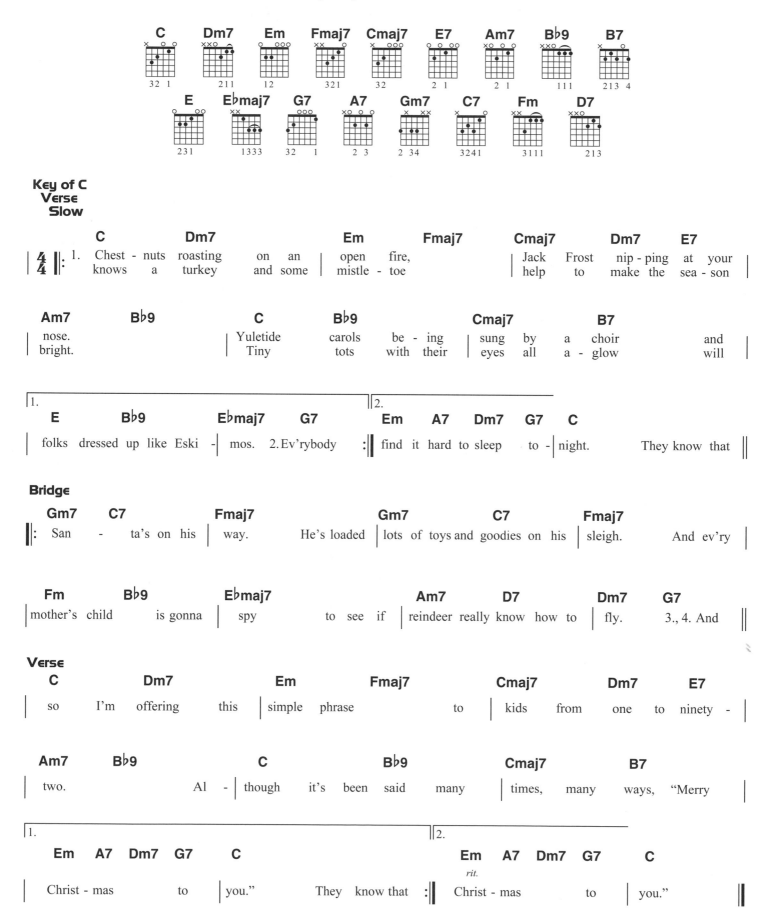

Christmas Time Is Here

from A CHARLIE BROWN CHRISTMAS
Words by Lee Mendelson
Music by Vince Guaraldi

Gmaj7   F7#11   C#m7b5   Bm7   Am7   C/D   Ebmaj7   Ab7#11   E7   D7

Key of G
Verse
Slow

Gmaj7   **F7#11**   **Gmaj7**
3/4 |: 1. Christmas time   is | here, | happi - ness   and
     2. Snowflakes   in   the | air, | carols   ev - 'ry -
     4., 5. *Instrumental*

F7#11   **C#m7b5**   **Bm7**
| cheer. | Fun   for   all   that | children   call   their
| where. | Old - en   times   and | ancient   rhymes   of

Am7   **C/D**   **1.** **Gmaj7**   **2.** **Gmaj7**
| fa - v'rite   time   of | year.   :| share.
| love   and   dreams to | | *Instrumental ends*

Bridge

Ebmaj7   **Ab7#11**   **Ebmaj7**   **Ab7#11**
| Sleighbells   in   the | air, | beauty   ev'ry - | where. |

Bm7   **E7**   **Am7**   **D7**
| Yuletide   by   the | fireside   and | joyful   mem'ries | there. |

Verse

Gmaj7   **F7#11**   **Gmaj7**
| 3., 6. Christmas time   is | here, | we'll   be   drawing |

F7#11   **C#m7b5**   **Bm7**
| near. | Oh,   that   we   could | always   see   such |

                          To Coda ⊕   *D.C. al Coda*   ⊕ **Coda**
                                                   (take repeat)

Am7   **C/D**   **Gmaj7**   **Gmaj7**
| spirit   through   the | year.   ‖ | year.   ‖

Do You Hear What I Hear

Words and Music by Noel Regney and Gloria Shayne

C   B♭   G   F   Am   Em   E   Dm

Key of C
Intro
Moderately

C	B♭ C		B♭ C
4/4			1. Said the

✵ Verse

C		B♭ C	
night wind to the little	lamb,	do you see what I see?	
little lamb to the shepherd	boy,	do you hear what I hear?	

3., 4. *See additional lyrics*

		B♭ C	
(Do you see what I see?)	Way up in the sky, little	lamb,	
(Do you hear what I hear?)	Ring-ing through the sky, shepherd	boy,	

		Am	
do you see what I see?	(Do you see what I see?) A	star, a star,	
do you hear what I hear?	(Do you hear what I hear?) A	song, a song,	

4th time, To Coda ✛

Em		F G	E
danc-ing in the night, with a	tail as big as a	kite,	with a
high a-bove the tree, with a	voice as big as the	sea,	with a

1., 2.　　　　　**3.**

D.S. al Coda

F G C	B♭ C	C
tail as big as a | kite.	2. Said the	4. Said the
voice as big as the | sea.	3. Said the	

✛ Coda

F C	Dm G C	B♭ C	B♭ C
bring us	goodness and | light.		

Additional Lyrics

3. Said the shepherd boy to the mighty king,
   Do you know what I know? (Do you know what I know?)
   In your palace warm, mighty king,
   Do you know what I know? (Do you know what I know?)
   A Child, a Child shivers in the cold,
   Let us bring Him silver and gold,
   Let us bring Him silver and gold.

4. Said the king to the people ev'rywhere,
   Listen to what I say! (Listen to what I say!)
   Pray for peace, people ev'rywhere,
   Listen to what I say! (Listen to what I say!)
   The Child, the Child, sleeping in the night,
   He will bring us goodness and light,
   He will bring us goodness and light.

Christmas Wrapping

Words and Music by Chris Butler

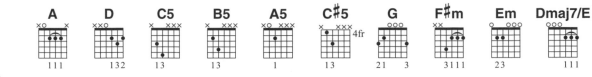

A	D	C5	B5	A5	C#5	G	F#m	Em	Dmaj7/E

Key of A
Verse
Moderately fast

A

$\frac{4}{4}$

1. Bah! Hum - bug! No, that's too strong 'cause it is my fa - v'rite hol - i - day. But
2. Cal - en - dar pic - ture, fro - zen land - scape chilled this room for twen - ty - four days.
3. Hard - ly dash - ing through the snow 'cause I bun - dled up too tight,
4. A. and P. has pro - vi - ded me with the world's small - est tur - key. Al -

D   **C5**   **B5**

all this year's been a bus - y blur. Don't think I have the en - er - gy to
Ev - er - greens, spar - kl - ing snow; get this win - ter o - ver with! Flash - back to
last min - ute have - to dos, a few cards, a few calls be - cause it's
read - y in the ov - en, nice and hot. Oh, damn! Guess what I for - got! So

A

add to my al - read - y mad rush just 'cause this is the sea - son. The
spring - time, saw him a - gain. Would - 've been good to go for lunch.
R. S. V. P. No thanks, no par - ty lights, it's
on with the boots, back out in the snow to the on - ly all - night gro - cer - y. When

D   **C5**   **B5**

per - fect gift for me would be com - pletions and con - nec - tions left from
Could - n't a - gree we're both free. We tried, we said we'd keep in touch.
Christ - mas Eve, gon - na re - lax, turned down all of my in - vites.
what to my won - der - ing eyes should ap - pear in the line is that guy I've been chas - ing all year!

A

last year, ski - shop en - coun - ter, most in - t'rest - ing.
Did - n't of course till sum - mer - time. Out to the beach to his boat, could I join him?
Last fall I had a night to my - self, same guy called, Hal - low - een par - ty,
"Spend - ing this one a - lone," he said, "Need a break; this year's been cra - zy." I

D   **C5**   **B5**

Had his num - ber, but nev - er the time. Most of eigh - ty - one passed a - long those lines. So,
No, this time it was me, sun - burn in the third de - gree.
wait - ed all night for him to show, this time his car would - n't go. For -
said, "Me too, but why are you... you mean you for - got cran - ber - ries, too? Then

A

deck those halls, trim those trees, raise up cups of Christ - mas cheer.
Now the cal - en - dar's just one page, of course, I am ex - cit - ed. To -
get it, it's cold, it's get - ting late, trudge on home to cel - e - brate in a
sud - den - ly we laughed and laughed, caught on to what was hap - pen - ing. That

D .... **B5** .... **A5** ... **C#5** ... **A5**

I just need to catch my breath, Christ - mas by my - self this

night's the night, I've set my mind not to ¾ do too much a - bout this

qui - et way, un - wind, do - ing Christ - mas right this ¼

Christ - mas mag - ic's brought this tale to a ver - y hap - py end -

1., 3. | 2., 4.

A

¼ year.

it.

time.

ing.

1., 3.

Interlude

D **G** **D** **G** **D** **G** **D** **G** **D**

2., 4.

To Coda ⊕

D **G** **F#m** **Em** **Dmaj7/E**

²⁄₄ Merry ⁴⁄₄

Chorus

A

⁴⁄₄ Christmas! Merry Christmas! But I | think I'll miss this one this year. Merry |

Christmas! Merry Christmas! But I | think I'll miss this one this year. Merry |

Christmas! Merry Christmas! But I | think I'll miss this one this year. Merry |

D.C. al Coda
(take repeats)

Christmas! Merry Christmas! But I ¾ think I'll miss this one this year. ⁴⁄₄

⊕ **Coda**

Repeat and fade

A

⁴⁄₄ Christmas! Merry Christmas! | Couldn't miss this one this year! Merry :||

Do They Know It's Christmas?
(Feed the World)

Words and Music by Bob Geldof and Midge Ure

C   F   G   Dm   Am

Key of C
Intro
Moderately

C
| 4/4 | | | | It's Christmas ||

Verse

F   G   C
| time, | there's no need to | be afraid. | At Christmas |

F   G   C
| time, we let in light and we | banish shade. | And in our world |

F   G   C   F
| of plen- ty, we can | spread a smile of joy. | Throw your arms |

Dm   G   C
| around the world | at Christmas time. | But say a |

F   G   C
| prayer, | to pray for the | other ones. | At Christmas |

F   G   C
| time, it's | hard but, when you're | having fun, | there's a |

F   G   C   F
| world outside your win- dow, and it's a | world of dread and fear | where the |

Dm   G   C   F
| only water | flowing is the | bitter sting of | tears. And the |

Dm	**G**	**C**	**F**
Christmas bells that ring	there are the	clanging chimes of doom.	Well, to -

Dm	**G**	**C**	
night thank God it's them	instead of	you.	And there

F	**G**	**C**	
won't be snow in Af -	rica this Christ	- mas time.	The

F	**G**	**C**	
greatest gift they'll	get this year is life.	Oh.	Where

F	**G**	**C**	**F**
nothing ever grows,	no rain or rivers flow,		

Dm	**G**	**C**	**F** **C**
do they know it's	Christmas time at	all?	

Bridge

Am	**G**	**Am**
Here's to you, raise a	glass for ev'ryone;	here's to them under -

G	**F**	**G**
neath that burning sun.	Do they know it's	Christmas time at

2nd time, Voc. tacet

C	**F** **C**	**F** **C**	**Dm**
all?			

Outro

C	**F** **C**	**F** **C**	**Dm**
Feed the	world.		

Repeat and fade

C	**F** **C**	**F** **C**	**Dm**
{ Feed } { gain. } the	world,	let them know it's	Christmas time a -

Feliz Navidad

Music and Lyrics by José Feliciano

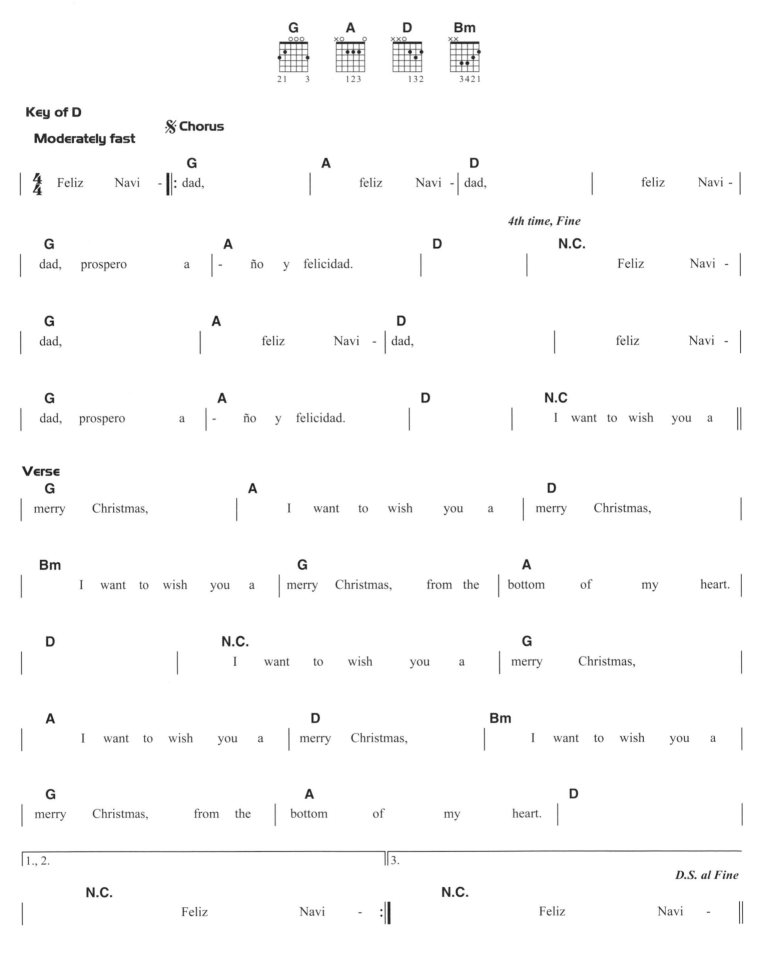

Frosty the Snow Man

Words and Music by Steve Nelson and Jack Rollins

C   F   A7   Dm7   G7   Em   G   D7

Key of C
Verse
Moderately slow, in 2

C
1. Frosty the | snow man was a | jol - ly, hap - py | soul, with a |
3. Frosty the | snow man knew the | sun was hot that | day, so he |

F ... **C** ... **A7** ... **Dm7** ... **G7** ... **C** ... **G7**
corn - cob pipe and a | but - ton nose and two | eyes made out of | coal. |
said, "Let's run and we'll | have some fun now be - | fore I melt a - | way." |

C ... **F** ... **C**
Fros - ty the | snow man is a | fairy tale, they | say; he was |
Down to the | vil - lage with a | broomstick in his | hand; run - ning |

F ... **C** ... **A7** ... **Dm7** ... **G7** ... **C**
made of snow, but the | chil - dren know how he | came to life one | day. There |
here and there, all a - | round the square, say - in', | "Catch me if you | can." He |

Bridge

F ... **Em** ... **Dm7** ... **G7** ... **C**
must have been some | mag - ic in that | old silk hat they | found, for |
led them down the | streets of town right | to the traf - fic | cop, and he |

G ... **D7** ... **G7**
when they placed it | on his head, he be | - gan to dance a - | round. 2. Oh, |
on - ly paused a | mo - ment when he | heard him hol - ler, | "Stop!" 4. For |

Verse

C ... **F** ... **C**
Frosty the | snow man was a - | live as he could | be, and the |
Frosty the | snow man had to | hur - ry on his | way, but he |

F ... **C** ... **A7** ... **Dm7** ... **G7** ... **C**
chil - dren say he could | laugh and play just the | same as you and | me. |
waved good - bye, say - in', | "Don't you cry, I'll be | back a - gain some - | day." |

Outro

C ... **G7**
Thumpety, thump, thump, | thumpety, thump, thump, | look at Frosty | go. |

C
Thumpety, thump, thump, | thumpety, thump, thump, | over the hills of | snow. |

Grandma Got Run Over by a Reindeer

Words and Music by Randy Brooks

E   A   B7   D   C#m   G#m   E7

Key of E
Chorus
Moderately

E
4/4 :|| Grandma got run over by a | reindeer | walking home from our house Christmas | Eve. | |

To Coda ⊕

E   B7   E   D   A
| You can say there's no such thing as | Santa,   but | as for me and Grandpa, we be - | lieve. ||

Verse

E   B7   E
1. She'd been drink - ing too much	eggnog	and we begged her not to	go.
2. Now, we're all so proud of	Grandpa.	He's been tak - ing this so	well.
3. Now, the goose is on the	table,	and the pud - ding made of	fig.

A   B7   E
But she for - got her med - i - cation, and she	stag - gered out the door in - to the	snow.
See him in there watch-ing	football, drink - ing	beer and play - ing cards with cous - in	Mel.
And the blue and sil - ver	candles that would	just have matched the hair in Grand-ma's	wig.

C#m   G#m   B7
When we found her Christ-mas	morning	at the scene of the at -
It's not Christ-mas with - out	Grandma.	All the fam - 'ly's dressed in
I've warned all my friends and	neighbors.	Bet - ter watch out for your -

E   E7   A
tack,	she had hoof - prints on her	forehead, and in -
black,	and we just can't help but	wonder: should we
selves.	They should nev - er give a	license to a

1., 2.   **3.**   *D.C. al Coda*

B7   E   E
| crim - i - nat - ing Claus marks on her | back. | elves. :|| |
| o - pen up her gifts or send them | back? |
| man who drives a sleigh and plays with |

⊕ **Coda**

Outro-Chorus

E   E   A
| lieve. || Grandma got run over by a | reindeer | walking home from our house Christmas | Eve. | |

E   B7   E B7 E
| You can say there's no such thing as | Santa, but | as for me and Grandpa, we be - | lieve. | ||

Have Yourself a Merry Little Christmas

from MEET ME IN ST. LOUIS
Words and Music by Hugh Martin and Ralph Blane

G   Em7   Am7   D7   Bm7   B7   E7   A7

G7   Cmaj7   Cm(maj7)   Gmaj7   C#m7♭5   F#7   D

Key of G
Verse
Slow

G	Em7		Am7	D7	G	Em7	Am7	D7	
4/4 1. Have your - self a	merry little Christmas,	let your heart be	light.						

Bm7	Em7		Am7	D7	B7	E7	A7	D7	
From now on our	troubles will be out of	sight.							

G	Em7		Am7	D7	G	Em7	Am7	D7	
Have your - self a	merry little Christmas,	make the Yuletide	gay.						

Bm7	Em7		Am7	B7	Em7	G7	
From now on our	troubles will be miles a -	way.					

Bridge

Cmaj7	Cm(maj7)		Bm7		Am7	D7	Gmaj7	
Here we are as in	olden days, happy	golden days of	yore.					

C#m7♭5	F#7		Bm7		D	A7	D7	
Faithful friends who are	dear to us gather	near to us once	more.					

Verse

G	Em7		Am7	D7	G	Em7	Am7	D7	
2. Through the years we	all will be to - gether,	if the fates al -	low.						

Bm7	Em7		Am7	B7	Em7	G7		
Hang a shining	star upon the highest	bough,		and				

Cmaj7		Am7	D7	G	
have yourself a	merry little Christmas	now.			

Happy Xmas
(War Is Over)

Written by John Lennon and Yoko Ono

A	Bm	E	D	Em	G
1 2 3	3 4 2 1	2 3 1	1 3 2	1 2	2 1 3

Key of A
Verse
Slow, in 2

A			**Bm**	
6/8 1. And so this is	Christmas	and what have you	done?	Another year

E		**A**		
over,	a new one just be -	gun.	And so this is

D		**Em**		
Christmas,	I hope you have	fun,	the near and the

A		**D**		
dear one,	the old and the	young.	A very merry

𝄋 **Chorus**

G		**A**		
‖: Christmas	and a happy new	year.	Let's hope it's a

3rd time, To Coda ⊕

Em	**G**	**D**	**E**	
good one	without any	fear.	2. And so this is	
			3. And so this is ‖	

Verse

A			**Bm**	
Christmas	for weak and for	strong,	the rich and the
Christmas	and what have we	done?	An - oth - er year
(War is	o - ver	if you	want it.

E		**A**		
poor ones,	the road is so	long.	And so, happy
o - ver,	a new year just be -	gun.	And so happy
War is	o - ver	now.	

D					**Em**	

Christmas | for   black   and   for | white, | for   yel - low   and
Christmas, | we   hope   you   have | fun,   if   you | want   it. | the   near   and   the |
| War   is | o   -   ver

2nd time, D.S. al Coda

A					**D**	

red   ones, | let's   stop   all   the | fight. ⎫ | A   very   merry   :‖
dear   ones, | the   old   and   the | young. ⎬ |
| War   is | o   -   ver | now. ⎭

⊕ **Coda**

                                                      Outro

E		**A**				**Bm**	

| ‖ War   is | o   -   ver | if   you |

	E			**A**	

| want   it. | War   is | o   -   ver | now. | ‖

Here Comes Santa Claus
(Right Down Santa Claus Lane)

Words and Music by Gene Autry and Oakley Haldeman

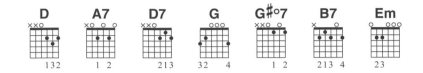

Key of D
Verse
Moderately fast

D   **A7**

| 4/4 |: 1.–4. Here comes Santa Claus! | Here comes Santa Claus! | Right down Santa Claus | Lane. |

                                                                        D   **D7**

Vix - en and Blitz - en and	all his rein - deer are	pull - ing on the	reins.
He's got a bag that's	filled with toys for the	boys and girls a -	gain.
He does - n't care if you're	rich or poor, he	loves you just the	same.
He'll come a - round when	chimes ring out that it's	Christ - mas morn a -	gain.

G   **G#°7**   **D**   **B7**   **Em**   **A7**   **D**   **D7**

Bells are ring - ing,	chil - dren sing - ing	all is	mer - ry and	bright.	So
Hear those sleigh bells	jin - gle jan - gle,	oh, what a	beau - ti - ful	sight.	So
San - ta knows we're	all God's chil - dren,	that makes	ev - 'ry - thing	right.	So
Peace on earth will	come to all if	we just	fol - low the	light.	So

G   **G#°7**   **D**   **B7**

hang your stockings	and	say your	pray'rs,	
jump in bed,	and	cover your	head,	'cause
fill your hearts	with	Christ - mas	cheer,	
let's give thanks to the	Lord a -	bove,	

| **1., 2., 3.** | | | | **4.** |

Em   **A7**   **D**   **D**

| Santa   Claus   comes   to - | night. | :|| night. |

A Holly Jolly Christmas

Music and Lyrics by Johnny Marks

C   Cmaj7   G7   F   Em   Dm   Am   D7

Key of C

Verse
Moderately fast

| | C   Cmaj7 | C | | G7 |
| 4/4 1. Have a | :(3.) holly jolly | Christmas, it's the | best time of the | year. | |

| I don't know if | there'll be snow, but | have a cup of | cheer. Have a |

| Cmaj7 | C | | G7 |
| holly jolly | Christmas, and when | you walk down the | street, |

| say hello to | friends you know and | ev'ryone you | meet. ‖

Bridge

| F | | Em | F | | C |
| Oh, ho, the | mistletoe | hung where you can | see. |

| Dm | Am | | D7 | | G7 |
| Somebody | waits for you; | kiss her once for | me.   2., 4. Have a ‖

Verse

| C   Cmaj7 | C | | G7 |
| holly jolly | Christmas, and in | case you didn't | hear, |

| | C | | D7   G7 |
| oh, by golly, have a | holly jolly | Christmas this |

| 1. | | 2. |
| C | | C |
| year.   3. Have a :‖ | year. ‖

I Heard the Bells on Christmas Day

Words by Henry Wadsworth Longfellow
Adapted by Johnny Marks
Music by Johnny Marks

G   C   D7   Em   F#7   Bm   Am   Bm7♭5   Em   A7

21 3   32 1   213   23   321   3421   231   2 1   2 1   2 3

Key of G

Verse
Moderately slow

	G	**C**	**D7**
4/4 1. I	heard the bells on	Christ - mas	Day, their
	in de - spair, I	bowed my	head: "There

Em		**F#7**	**Bm**	**Am**	**D7**
old fa - mil - iar	car - ols	play. And	wild	and sweet the
is no peace on	earth," I	said. "For	hate	is strong and

Bm7♭5	**E7**	**Am**	**E7**	**A7**	**D7**
words rep - peat, of	peace on	earth, good	will	to men. I
mocks the song of	peace on	earth, good	will	to men." Then

G		**C**	**D7**	**Em**
thought as now this	day had	come, the	bel - fries of all
pealed the bells more	loud and	deep; "God	is not dead, nor

F#7	**Bm**	**Am**	**D7**	**Bm7♭5**	**E7**
Chris - ten - dom had	rung	so long the un -	bro - ken song of
doth He sleep. The	wrong	so shall fail, the	right pre - vail with

1.

Am	**E7**	**D7**	**G**
peace on earth, good	will	to men. 2. And
peace on earth, good		

2.

| **D7** | **G** |
| will | to men." |

I Wonder as I Wander

By John Jacob Niles

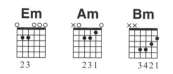

Key of Em

Slow   **Verse**

Em   **Am**   **Em**

3/4   1. I   ‖: (1., 4.) wonder   as   I | wander   out   'twas | un - der   the |
            Mary   birthed   had | Jesus,   wanted for | in   a   cow's |
            Jesus   had | wanted   for | an - y   wee |

Am   **Em**   **Am**   **Em**

sky   how | Je - sus   the | Sav - ior   did | come   for   to |
stall,   with | shep - herds   and | wise   men and | an - gels   and |
thing,   a | star   in   the | sky   or   a | bird   on   the |

die: To | save   low - ly | people   like | you   and   like |
all.   The | bless - ings of | Christmas from | heav - en   did |
wing,   or | all   of God's | angels   in | heav'n   for   to |

Bm   **Em**   **Am**   **Em**   **Bm**

I,   I | wonder   as   I | wan - der   out | un - der   the |
fall   and   the | weary   world could | woke   to the | Sav - ior's |
sing,   He | surely   could | have   it 'cause | He   was   the |

1., 2., 3. | **4.**

Em   **Em**

sky.   sky.
call.   2. When   :‖
King.   3. If
               4. I

I'll Be Home for Christmas

Words and Music by Kim Gannon and Walter Kent

G   G°7   Am7   D7   Bm11   E7♭9   Am   Em   A7   Am7♭5   E7

32 4   1324   2 1   213   1 2   2 3   231   23   2 3   2 3   2 1

Key of G
Verse
  Moderately slow

G		**G°7**		**Am7**		**D7**	
4/4 ‖: 1., 3. I'll	be	home	for	Christmas,			

Bm11		**E7♭9**		**Am**			
you	can	count	on	me.			

		D7		**G**		**Em**	
Please	have	snow	and	mistle	-	toe	and

A7				**Am7**		**D7**	
presents		on	the	tree.			‖

Verse

G		**G°7**		**Am7**		**D7**	
2., 4. Christmas		Eve	will	find	me		

Bm11		**E7♭9**		**Am**			
where	the	lovelight		gleams.			

		Am7♭5		**G**		**E7**	
I'll	be	home	for	Christ	-	mas,	if

1.

Am7		**D7**		**G**		**D7**	
only		in	my	dreams.			:‖

2.

G			
dreams.			

It's Beginning to Look Like Christmas

By Meredith Willson

G · C · B7 · E7 · Am7 · D7 · D · A7 · A#°7 · Em

Key of G

% **Verse**

Moderately (♩♩ = ♩♪)

G · **C** · **G** · **B7**
4/4 1. It's be - (2.) ginning to look a lot like | Christmas | ev'ry - where you |

C · **E7** · **Am7** · **D7** · **G**
| go. { Take a | look in the five and ten, | glis-ten-ing once a - gain, with |
{ There's a | tree in the grand ho - tel, | one in the park as well, the |

D · **A7** · **D7** · **G** · **C**
| candy canes and silver lanes a - | glow. It's be - | ginning to look a lot like |
| sturdy kind that doesn't mind the | snow. It's be - | ginning to look a lot like |

G · **B7** · **C** · **E7**
| Christmas, | toys in ev - 'ry | store. But the |
| Christmas, | soon the bells will | start. And the |

To Coda ⊕

Am7 · **A#°7** · **G** · **E7** · **Am7** · **D7**
| pret - ti - est sight to see is the | holly that will be on your | own front |
| thing that will make them ring is the | carol that you sing right with - | in your |

Bridge

G · **B7**
| door. A pair of ‖ hop - a - long boots and a pistol that shoots is the |

Em · **A7** · **D**
| wish of Barney and Ben. | Dolls that will talk and will go for a walk is the | hope of Janice and Jen. And |

D.S. al Coda · ⊕ **Coda**

D7 · **G**
| Mom and Dad can hardly wait for | school to start again. 2. It's be - ‖ | heart. ‖

Jingle Bell Rock

Words and Music by Joe Beal and Jim Boothe

Chords: C Cmaj7 C#°7 Dm G7 G7#5 F F#°7 D7 A7 Fm

Key of C
Verse
Moderately

C   Cmaj7   C   C#°7   Dm   G7
4/4 1. Jingle bell, jingle bell, | jingle bell rock, | jingle bells swing and | jingle bells ring. |

Dm   G7   Dm   G7   Dm   G7#5
| Snowin'   and blowin'   up | bushels   of   fun; | now the jingle hop | has begun. ‖

Verse

C   Cmaj7   C   C#°7   Dm   G7
‖: 2., 4. Jingle bell, jingle bell, | jingle bell rock, | jingle bells chime in | jingle bell time. |

Dm   G7   Dm   G7   Dm   G7   C
| Dancin'   and prancin'   in | Jingle Bell Square | in   the   frosty | air.   What a ‖

Bridge

F   F#°7   C
| bright   time,   it's the | right   time   to | rock   the   night   a - | way.   Jingle |

D7   G7
| bell   time   is a | swell   time | to   go   glidin' in the | one - horse sleigh. ‖

Verse

C   Cmaj7   C   A7
| 3., 5. Giddyap,   jingle horse, | pick up your feet, | jingle around   the | clock. |

F   Fm | 1. | D7   G7   C
| Mix   and   mingle in the | jinglin'   beat, | that's   the   jingle   bell | rock. :‖

| 2. |
D7   G7   D7   G7   D7   G7   C
| that's the jingle bell, | that's the jingle bell, | that's the jingle bell | rock. | ‖

Last Christmas

Words and Music by George Michael

C   Am7   Dm7   G7

32 1   2 1   211   32 1

Key of C
Chorus
Moderately

C
‖ 4/4 ‖: Last Christmas I | gave you my heart, but the | very next day you | gave it away. |

Dm7   **G7**
| This year, to | save me from tears, I'll | give it to someone spe | - cial. |

C   **Am7**
| Last Christmas I | gave you my heart, but the | very next day you | gave it away. |

Dm7   **G7**
| This year, to | save me from tears, I'll | give it to someone spe | - cial. ‖

Verse

C   **Am7**
| 1. Once bitten and | twice shy, I keep my dis - | tance, but
| 2. A crowd - ed room, | friends with tired eyes. | I'm hid - ing from you
| 3. *Lead voc. ad lib.*

                          Dm7
| tears still catch my eye. | Tell me, ba - by, do you rec - ognize me? |
| and your soul of ice. | My god, I thought you were | some - one to rely on. |

G7   **C**
| Well, it's been a year. It | doesn't sur - prise me. | *Happy Christ - mas.* I |
| Me, I guess I was a | shoulder to cry on, a | face on a lover with a |

                    Am7   **Dm7**
| wrapped it up and sent it | with a note say - ing, "I | love you." I meant it. | Now I know what a fool |
| fire in his heart, a | man un - der cov - er but you | tore me a - | part.

|1. |2.
                                              D.C. and fade on Verse

G7
| I've been, but if you | kissed me now I | know you'd fool me again. | :‖ fool me again. ‖
| Oo, now I've | found a real love. You'll nev - er

Let It Snow! Let It Snow! Let It Snow!

Words by Sammy Cahn
Music by Jule Styne

D   A7   A   E7   Em   B7   Bm7   F#7

Key of D

Verse
Moderately

D ... **A7** ... **D** ... **A** ... **E7**

4/4 1. Oh, the ‖: weather out - side is | frightful, but the | fire is so de -
doesn't show signs of stopping, and I brought some corn for

A ... **Em** ... **B7** ... **Em**

lightful, and | since we've no place to | go, ⎫ let it |
popping. The lights are turned way down low; ⎭

A7 ... **D** ... **D**

1.
2.

snow, let it snow, let it | snow! 2. It :‖ snow! When we ‖

Bridge

A ... **Bm7** ... **E7** ... **A**

‖: finally kiss good - | night, how I'll | hate going out in the | storm! But if |

F#7 ... **B7** ... **E7** ... **A** ... **A7**

you really hold me | tight, all the way home I'll be | warm. 3., 4. The ‖

Verse

D ... **A7** ... **D** ... **A** ... **E7** ... **A**

fire is slowly | dying, and, my | dear, we're still good | - byeing, but as |

Em ... **B7** ... **Em** ... **A7** ... **D**

1.
long as you love me | so, let it | snow, let it snow, let it | snow! When we :‖

2.

A7 ... **D**

snow, let it | snow, let it | snow! |

The Little Drummer Boy

Words and Music by Harry Simeone, Henry Onorati and Katherine Davis

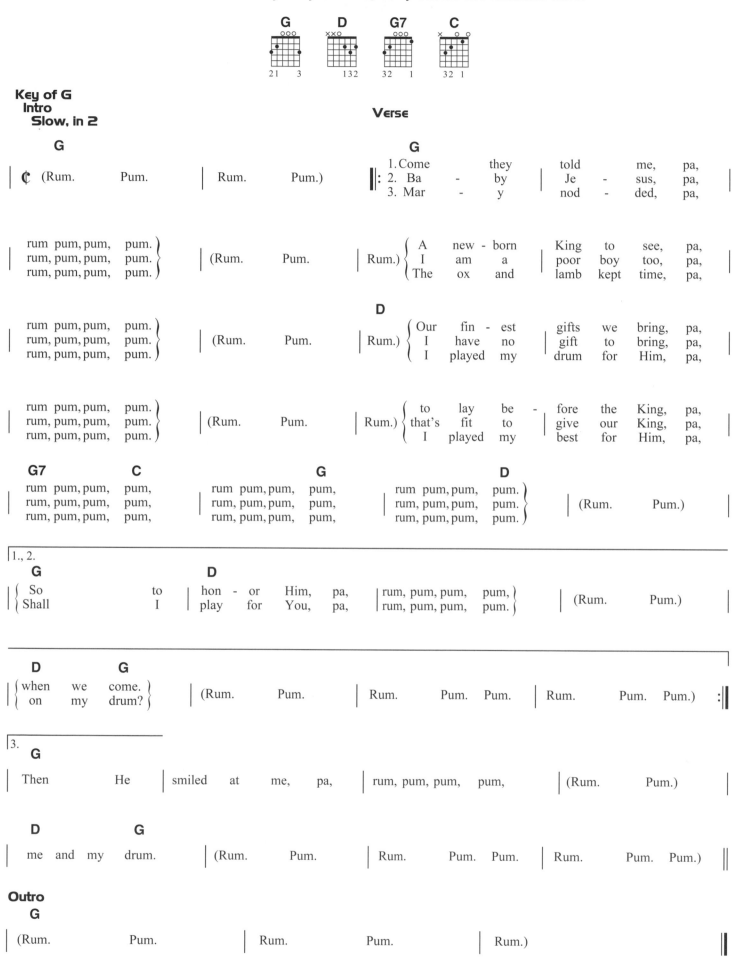

A Marshmallow World

Words by Carl Sigman
Music by Peter De Rose

G   D7   A7   D   G7   C

Key of G

Verse

Moderately fast (♩♩ = ♩♪³)

G

| It's a | marshmallow world in the | winter when the | snow comes to cover the |
| | marshmallow clouds be-ing | friendly in the | arms of the ever-green |

D7   **G**

| ground. It's the | time for play, it's a | whipped-cream day. I |
| trees. And the | sun is red like a | pump-kin head, it's |

1.
A7   **D7**   **2.** **A7**   **D7**   **G**

| wait for it the whole year | round. Those are :‖ shining so your nose won't | freeze. The ‖ |

Bridge

G7   **C**   **G7**   **C**

| world is your snow ball; | see how it grows. | That's how it goes, when-ever it snows. The |

A7   **D**   **A7**   **D7**

| world is your snow ball; | just for a song, get | out and roll it a- | long. It's a ‖ |

Outro-Verse

G   **D7**

| yum-yummy world made for | sweet hearts. Take a | walk with your favorite | girl. It's a |

G   **A7**   **D7**   **G**

| sugar date. What if | spring is late? In | winter, it's a marshmallow | world. ‖ |

Merry Christmas, Baby

Words and Music by Lou Baxter and Johnny Moore

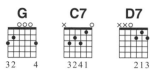

Key of G
Verse
Slow (♫ = ♩♪)

| **G** | **C7** | **G** |
| 4/4 1. Merry Christmas, baby, | you sure did treat me | nice. | | |

| **C7** | | **G** |
| Merry Christmas, baby, | you sure did treat me | nice. | | Gave me a |

| **D7** | | **G** |
| diamond ring for Christmas, | now I'm livin' in para - | dise. | | 2. Well I'm |

Verse

| **G** | **C7** | **G** |
| feelin' mighty fine, | got good music on my radio. | | | Well, I'm |

| **C7** | | **G** |
| feelin' mighty fine, | got good music on my radio. | | | Well, I |

| **D7** | | **G** |
| want to kiss you, baby, | while you're standin' 'neath the mistletoe. | | | Saint |

Outro-Verse

| **G** | **C7** **G** | **C7** **G** |
| Nick came down the chimney 'bout | half - past three, | left | all these pretty presents that you |

| **C7** **G** | **C7** | **G** |
| see before me. Merry | Christmas, litle baby, | you sure been good to | me. | |

| | **D7** | |
| | I haven't | had a drink this mornin', but I'm | |

| | **G** **C7** **G** | |
| all lit up like a Christmas | tree. | |

Mary, Did You Know?

Words and Music by Mark Lowry and Buddy Greene

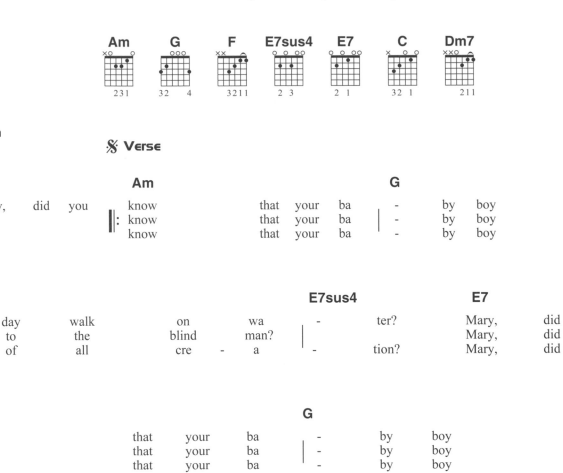

Key of Am

Slow

%. **Verse**

Am   G

1. Mary, did you ‖: know   that your ba - by boy   would
know   that your ba - by boy   will give
know   that your ba - by boy   is Lord

F   E7sus4   E7

one day walk on wa - ter?   Mary, did you
sight to the blind man? - Mary, did you
of all cre - a - tion? Mary, did you

Am   G

know   that your ba - by boy   would
know   that your ba - by boy   would
know   that your ba - by boy   would

F   E7sus4   E7

save our sons and daugh - ters?   Did you know
calm a storm with His hand? Did you know
one day rule the na - tions? - Did you know

F   G

that your ba - by boy   has
that your ba - by boy   has
that your ba - by boy   was

C   G   Am

come to make you new?   This
walked to where an - gels trod? When you
heav - en's per - fect lamb? That the sleep -

To Coda ⊕

Dm7

child that you de - liv - ered   will
kiss your lit - tle ba - by, you've kissed the
- ing Child you're hold - ing is the

	1. **E7**	2. **E7**
soon de - liv - er you?	2. Mary, did you :
the face of God?	

Interlude

Am	**G**	**F**	**E7sus4** **E7**

Am	**G**	**F**	**E7sus4** **E7**
			The

Bridge

F	**G**	**Am**
blind will see, the	deaf will hear, the	dead will live again.

C	**F**	**G**
The	lame will leap, the	dumb will speak the

D.S. al Coda

Am	**E7**	
praises of The Lamb.		3. Mary, did you

⊕ Coda

E7sus4	**E7**	**Am**	**G**
great	"I	AM?"	

F	**E7sus4** **E7**	**Am**	**G**

F	**E7sus4** **E7**	**Am**	
		Mary, did you	know?

The Most Wonderful Time of the Year

Words and Music by Eddie Pola and George Wyle

C   Am7   Dm7   G7   Dm   Em   F   F#°7   Gm7   Fm6   Ebmaj7   G

Key of C

Fast

𝄋 Verse

3/4 1. It's the | C most | Am7 wonderful | Dm7 time | G7 son of the |
               hap - | happiest | sea - | son of |

C year, | Am7 | Dm7 | G7 with the | Dm7 kids jingle |
    all, | | | with those | hol - iday |

G7 belling and | Em ev - 'ryone | Am7 telling you, | F "Be of good | cheer." |
   greetings and | gay happy | meetings when | friends come to | call. |

F#°7 | | It's the | C most | Am7 wonderful | Dm7 time |
                It's the | hap - | happiest | sea - |

1.

G7 son of the | C year. | Am7 | Dm7 | G7 2. It's the :||

2.

Gm7 all. | | C | There'll be |

Bridge

||: F parties for | F#°7 hosting, marsh - | mallows for | C |

Am7 toasting and | Dm7 caroling | G7 out in the | C snow. | There'll be |

Fm6   **E♭maj7**

| scary | ghost | stories | and | tales | of | the | glories | of |

Fm6   **G**   **N.C.**

| Christmases | long, long a - | go. | | | 3., 4. It's the |

Verse

C   **Am7**   **Dm7**   **G7**

| most | wonderful | time | | of | the |

C   **Am7**   **Dm7**   **G7**   **Dm7**

| year. | | | There'll be | much mistle - |

G7   **Em**   **Am7**   **F**

| toeing and | hearts will be | glowing when | loved ones are |

                        F♯°7   **C**   **Am7**

| near. | | It's the | most | wonderful |

1.

Dm7   **G7**   **C**   **Gm7**   **C**

| time | of the | year! | | | There'll be :‖

2.

Dm7   **G7**   **C**   **Am7**   **Dm7**

| time, | yes, the | most | wonderful | time, |

G7   **C**   **Am7**   **Dm7**

| oh, the | most | wonderful | time |

G7   **C**

| of the | year. | | | |

Nuttin' for Christmas

Words and Music by Roy C. Bennett and Sid Tepper

G   D7   C   A7   Em   Am   E7

Key of G
Chorus
Moderately fast

G
| 4/4 ‖: I'm gettin' | nuttin' for | Christmas, | | **D7** Mommy and |

| Daddy are | mad. | | **G** I'm gettin' | nuttin' for | Christmas |

To Coda ⊕

| **D7** 'cause | I ain't been | nuttin' but | **G** bad. | | 1., 2., 3. I ‖

Verse

G   **C**   **G**   **A7**   **D7**   **G**

broke my bat on	Johnny's head;	somebody snitched on	me. I
put a tack on	teacher's chair;	somebody snitched on	me. I
won't be see - ing	Santa Claus;	somebody snitched on	me. He

C   **G**   **A7**   **D7**   **G**

hid a frog in	sis - ter's bed;	somebody snitched on	me. I
tied a knot in	Su - sie's hair;	somebody snitched on	me. I
won't come vis - it	me be - cause	somebody snitched on	me.

C   **D7**   **G**

spilled some ink on	Mommy's rug,	I made Tom - my	eat a bug,
did a dance on	Mommy's plants,	climbed a tree and	tore my pants,
Next year, I'll be	going straight,	next year, I'll be	good, just wait,

Em   **A7**   **D7**

bought some gum with a	pen - ny slug;	somebody snitched on
filled the sug - ar	bowl with ants;	somebody snitched on
I'd start now but	it's too late;	somebody snitched on

1., 2. **G**		3. **G** *D.C. al Coda*
me. Oh,		‖ me. Oh, ‖
me. Oh,		

⊕ **Coda**

Outro
Am   **E7**

| So, you ‖ better be good, what - | ever you do, 'cause, |

Am   **E7**   **Am**   **D7**   **G**

| if you're bad, I'm | warning you: | you'll get | nuttin' for | Christmas. |

Please Come Home for Christmas

Words and Music by Charles Brown and Gene Redd

E   E7   A   A#°7   C#m   F#7   B7   Am   G#

Key of E

Moderately   **Verse**

$\frac{12}{8}$ 1. Bells will be ‖: ringing   the glad, glad | news,   oh, what a | Christmas   to have the
                    singing   "Si - lent | Night,"   Christ - mas | carols   by candle -

A#°7
| blues.   My ba - by's | gone,   I have no | friends   to wish me
| light. Please come home for | Christmas, please come home for | Christmas; if not for

1.
F#7   B7
| greetings   once a - | gain.   2. Choirs will be :‖

2.
F#7   B7
Christmas,   by New Year's

Bridge
E   E7   A   Am
| night.   Friends and re - ‖: lations   send salu - | tations |

E   E7   A
| sure   as the stars shine a - | bove.   This is | Christmas,   yes, Christmas, my

Am   F#7   B7
| dear,   the time of | year   to be with the one you | love.   3., 4. Then won't you ‖

Verse
E   E7   A
| tell   me you'll nevermore | roam,   Christmas and | New year   will find you at |

A#°7   E   G#   C#m   A
| home.   There'll be no more | sorrow,   no grief and | pain   'cause I'll be |

1.
E   B7   E
| happy, happy once   a - | gain.

2.
E7   E
Friends and re - :‖ gain.   ‖

River

Words and Music by Joni Mitchell

Gsus4   G   Em   D   C   Cmaj7   Am

Key of G

𝄋 Verse
Moderately

Gsus4   G   Gsus4   G
| 4/4 1. It's ‖: (1., 3.) coming   on   Christ - mas,   they're | cutting down   trees.   They're |
| tried hard   to   help   me, you know he | put   me   at   ease.   And he |

Gsus4   G   Gsus4   G
| putting up   rein - deer   and   singing | songs   of   joy   and peace. Oh, I |
| loved   me   so naughty, made me   weak | in   the knees.   Oh, I |

To Coda ⊕

Em
| wish   I   had   a   river | I   could   skate   a - |
| wish   I   had   a   river | I   could   skate   a - |

D
| way   on. | But |
| way   on. |

Gsus4   G   Gsus4   G
| it   don't   snow   here; | stays pretty green.   I'm gon - na |
| I'm so   hard   to handle.   I'm | selfish   and I'm sad. Now I've gone and |

Gsus4   G   Gsus4   G
| make a   lot of money,   then I'm gonna quit | this crazy   scene. ⎫ I |
| lost the best   baby that   I | ev -   er   had. Oh, ⎭ |

Em   **D**
| wish I had a river | I   could skate   a - | way   on. | I |

C   **D**   **G**

| wish I had a river   so   long, | I would | teach my   feet   to |

1.

C   **G**   **Am**   **G**

| fly. | | Oh, I | wish I had a   river |

D   **Cmaj7**   **C**

| I could   skate away | on. | I | made   my baby |

G   **Em**   **D**

| cry. | | | | | 2. He :‖

2.

Am

| | | | Oh,   I |

G   **D**   **Cmaj7**

| wish I had a river | I could   skate away | on. | I |

C   **G**   **Em**

| made   my   baby | say goodbye. | | |

D.S. al Coda

                              D

| | | | 3. It's ‖

Coda

D   **G**

| way | | on. | | ‖

Rudolph the Red-Nosed Reindeer

Music and Lyrics by Johnny Marks

C   Bm   Am   G   Em   A7   D7   D

Key of G
Intro
Freely

| | C | Bm | Am | G | C | Bm |
| | | | | | | |

4/4 You know | Dasher and Dancer and | Prancer and Vixen, | Comet and Cupid and |

| Am | G | Em | | | A7 | |

| Donner and Blitzen, | but do you re - | call the most | famous reindeer of |

Verse
Moderately fast (♫ = ♩♪³)

| D7 | | G | | | D7 | |

| all? ‖: 1., 3. Rudolph the red - nosed | reindeer | had a very shiny | nose,

| | | | | | G | |

| and if you ever | saw it, | you would even say it | glows.

| | | | | | D7 | |

| All of the other | reindeer | used to laugh and call him | names.

| | | | | | G | |

| They never let poor | Rudolph | join in any reindeer | games.

Bridge

| C | | G | | D7 | | G |

| Then one foggy | Christmas Eve, | Santa came to | say,

| D | | A7 | | D7 | |

| "Rudolph with your | nose so bright, | won't you guide my | sleigh tonight?"

Verse

| G | | | | | D7 |

| 2., 4. Then how the reindeer | loved him, | as they shouted out with | glee:

1.

| | | | | | G | |

| "Rudolph the red - nosed | reindeer, | you'll go down in histo - | ry!" :‖

2.

| | | | | G | |

| you'll go down in | histo - | ry!"

Santa Baby

By Joan Javits, Phil Springer and Tony Springer

C   Am   D7   G7   Dm   E7   A7

Key of C
Verse
Moderately slow (♫ = ♪♪)

C	Am	D7	G7	C	Am
4/4 1. Santa baby, just	slip a sable under the tree		for me;		
4. Santa honey, one	lit-tle thing I really need:		the deed		

D7	G7	C	Am	Dm	G7
been an awful good girl,	Santa baby, so	hurry down the chimney tonight.			
to a plati-num mine,	Santa baby, so	hurry down the chimney tonight.			

Verse

C	Am	Dm	G7	C	Am	D7	G7
				2. Santa baby, a	fifty - four con - vert-i-ble too,		
				5. Santa cutie, and	fill my stock - ing with a du-plex		

C	Am	D7	G7	C	Am
light blue.	I'll wait up for you dear,		Santa baby, so		
and cheques.	Sign your X on the line,		Santa cutie, and		

Bridge

Dm	G7	C	E7
hurry down the chimney tonight.			Think of all the
hurry down the chimney tonight.			Come and trim my

	A7
fun I've missed.	Think of all the fellas that I
Christ - mas tree	with some dec - o - rations bought at

	D7
haven't kissed.	Next year I could be just as good if
Tiffa - ny.	I really do be - lieve in you.

G7	N.C.
you check off my	Christ - mas list.
Let's see if you be -	lieve in me.

Verse

C	Am	D7	G7	C	Am
3. Santa baby, I	want a yacht, and real - ly that's not		a lot;		
6. Santa baby, for -	got to men - tion one lit-tle thing:		a ring.		

D7	G7	C	Am	Dm	G7
been an an - gel all year,	Santa baby, so	hurry down the chimney tonight.			
I don't mean on the phone,	Santa baby, so	hurry down the chimney tonight.			

1.		2.
C	G7	

Run Rudolph Run

Music and Lyrics by Johnny Marks and Marvin Brodie

Chorus

A | run, Rudolph, | D Santa's gotta make it to town. A | | |

D | Santa, tell him hurry, tell him | he can take the freeway down. A | | Run, |

[1.

E7 | run, Rudolph, 'cause I'm | reelin' like a merry - | go - round. A | 2. Said :||

[2.

Begin fade

Outro

A | A || | | | D | A | | ||

Fade out

49

Santa Claus Is Comin' to Town

Words by Haven Gillespie
Music by J. Fred Coots

C   F   Am   Dm   G7   C7   D7   G

Key of C

Verse

Moderately

|| C | F | C | F |
1. You |: better watch out,   you | better not   cry, | better not pout, I'm | telling you why: }
      little   tin   horns   and | little toy drums, | rooty toot toots and | rummy tum tums. }

| C   Am | Dm   G7 | C | G7
| Santa   Claus   is | comin'   to | town. | { 2. He's
                                                     5. With

Verse

| C | F | C | F
| making a   list   and | checking it twice, | gonna find   out   who's | naughty and   nice. }
| curly head dolls that | cuddle   and   coo, | ele - phants, boats and | kiddy cars, too. }

| C   Am | Dm   G7 | C
| Santa   Claus   is | comin'   to | town. | { He
                                                     The

Bridge

| C7 | F | C7 | F
| sees   you   when you're | sleep - ing.   He | knows when you're a - | wake.   He
| kids   in   girl   and | boy - land   will | have   a   ju - bi - | lee.   They're

| D7 | G | D7 | G
| knows   if   you've been | bad   or   good, so be | good   for goodness | sake. } 3., 6. Oh!   You
| gon - na build   a | toy - land town all a - | round the Christmas | tree. }

Verse

| C | F | C | F
| better watch out,   you | better not   cry, | better not pout, I'm | telling you why:

1.   2.

| C   Am | Dm   G7 | C
| Santa   Claus   is | comin'   to | town. | 4. With :||

Silver and Gold

Music and Lyrics by Johnny Marks

C   Am   Dm   G7   Em   D7   G   C7   F   A7   E♭°7

Key of C
Verse
Moderately

C			Am			Dm			G7		
3/4 Silver		and	gold,			silver		and	gold,		

C			Am			Dm			G7		
ev'ryone			wishes		for	silver		and	gold.		

C			Em			Am					
How	do	you	measure		its	worth,					

D7						G			G7		
just	by	the	pleasure		it	gives	here	on	earth?		

C			Am			Dm			G7		
Silver		and	gold,			silver		and	gold		

C			C7			F			A7		
mean	so	much	more	when	I	see					

Dm			E♭°7				C				
silver	and	gold	deco -	rations				on			

G			G7			C					
ev'ry			Christmas			tree.					

Silver Bells

from the Paramount Picture THE LEMON DROP KID
Words and Music by Jay Livingston and Ray Evans

G   C   D7   Am

Key of G
Chorus
Moderately

G		C	
3/4 ‖: Silver bells,		silver bells,	

D7		G	
it's Christmas	time in the	city.	

		C	
Ring - a - ling,		hear them ring,	

Fine

D7		G	
soon it will	be Christmas	Day.	1. Cit - y 2. Strings of ‖

Verse

G		C	Am
side - walks, busy	sidewalks dressed in	hol - i - day	style; in the
street lights, even	stoplights blink a	bright red and	green as the

D7		G	
air there's a	feel - ing of	Christmas.	Chil - dren
shop - pers rush	home with their	treasures.	Hear the

		C	Am
laugh - ing, peo - ple	pass - ing, meet - ing	smile af - ter	smile, and on
snow crunch, see the	kids bunch, this is	San - ta's big	scene, and a-

2nd time, D.C. al Fine

D7		G	D7
ev - 'ry street	corner you	hear:	:‖
bove all this	bustle you	hear:	

Copyright © 1950 Sony/ATV Music Publishing LLC
Copyright Renewed
All Rights Administered by Sony/ATV Music Publishing LLC, 424 Church Street, Suite 1200, Nashville, TN 37219
International Copyright Secured   All Rights Reserved

52

Somewhere in My Memory

from the Twentieth Century Fox Motion Picture HOME ALONE
Words by Leslie Bricusse
Music by John Williams

C   Cmaj7   F   Em   Dm   Fmaj7   G   D7   E7   Am

Key of C
Verse
Slow

C	Cmaj7		F	Em		Dm	Em	
4/4 Candles	in the		win - dow,			shadows	painting the	

Fmaj7	G		C	Cmaj7		F	Em	
ceil - ing,			gazing	at the		fire	glow,	

Bridge

F	C		Fmaj7	G		C	F	
feeling that	"gingerbread"		feel - ing.			Precious	moments,	

D7	G		E7	Am		Dm	G	
special	people,		happy	faces		I	can see.	

Outro-Verse

C	Cmaj7		F	Em		Dm	Em	
Somewhere	in my		mem - 'ry,			Christmas	joys all a-	

Fmaj7	G		C	Cmaj7		F	Em	
round	me,		living	in my		mem - 'ry		

F	C		F	Em		F	C	
all of the music,			all of the magic,			all of the fam'ly		

F	G		C	
home here		with	me.	

Sleigh Ride

Music by Leroy Anderson
Words by Mitchell Parish

C   Am7   Dm7   G7   F#m7   B7   E   Em7   A7

Dmaj7   Cadd9   Cmaj7   C#°7   B7/D#   E7   Am   G

Key of C

Moderately, in 2   %. **Verse**

N.C.		C Am7	Dm7 G7	C Am7	Dm7 G7
¢ 1. Just hear those	(3.) sleigh bells jingling,	ring - ting - tingling,	too.		Come on, it's

C Am7	Dm7 G7	C Am7	Dm7 G7
lovely weather for a	sleigh ride to-gether with	you.	Out - side the

C Am7	Dm7 G7	C Am7	Dm7 G7
snow is falling and	friends are calling, "Yoo	hoo."	Come on, it's

C Am7	Dm7 G7	C	
lovely weather for a	sleigh ride to-gether with	you.	Giddy -

Bridge

F#m7		B7 E	
yap, giddyyap, giddy -	yap, let's go,	let's look at the	show.

F#m7		B7 E	
We're riding in a	wonder - land of	snow.	Giddy -

Em7		A7 Dmaj7	
yap, giddyyap, giddy -	yap, it's grand	just holding your	hand.

Dm7		G7	
We're gliding a -	long with a song of a	wintery fairy -	land. 2., 4. Our cheeks are

Verse

C	Am7	Dm7	G7	C	Am7	Dm7	G7

| nice and rosy and | comfy, cozy are | we. | | We're snuggled |

C	Am7	Dm7	G7	C	Am7	Dm7	G7

| up to - gether like two | birds of a feather would | be. | | Let's take that |

C	Am7	Dm7	G7	C	Am7	Dm7	G7

| road be - fore us and | sing a chorus or | two. | | Come on, it's |

To Coda ⊕

C	Am7	Dm7	G7	C

| lovely weather for a | sleigh ride to - gether with | you. | | There's a ‖

Bridge

Cadd9   Cmaj7

‖: birthday party | at the home of | farm - er | Gray. It'll
happy feeling | noth - ing in the | world can | buy when they

| be the per - fect | ending of a | per - fect | day. We'll be
| pass a - round the | coffee and the | pump - kin | pie. It'll

1.

C♯°7   Dm7   B7/D♯   C   E7   Am

| singing the songs we | love to sing with -| out a sin - gle | stop at the |
| nearly be like a | pic - ture print by | Cur - ri - er and |

E   B7   E   N.C.   G   N.C.

| fireplace where we'll | watch the chestnuts | pop. | Pop, pop, pop! There's a :‖

2.

D.S. al Coda

Am7   Dm7   G7

| Ives. | These wonderful | things are the things we re -| member all through our | lives. 3.Just hear those ‖

⊕ **Coda**

Repeat and fade

C   Am7   Dm7   G7   C   Am7   Dm7   G7

‖: you. | | Lovely weather for a | sleigh ride to - gether with :‖

This Christmas

Words and Music by Donny Hathaway and Nadine McKinnor

Gmaj7　Em7　Fmaj7　D7　Bm7　E7　Am7　D7sus4　G　Cmaj7　C#m7b5　C#7b5

Key of G
Verse
Moderately slow

Gmaj7	Em7
4/4 1. Hang all the mis - tle - toe.	I'm gon - na get to know you
2. Pres - ents and cards are here.	My world is filled with cheer and

Fmaj7	Em7　D7　Gmaj7
better this Christ - mas.	And as we trim the tree,
you this Christ - mas.	And as I look a - round,

Em7	Fmaj7	Em7　D7
how much fun it's gonna be to - gether		this Christ - mas.} The
your eyes out - shine the town; they do,		this Christ - mas.}

Pre-Chorus

Bm7	E7
fireside is blazing bright.	We're

Am7	D7sus4
carolin' through the night	and this

Chorus

G	Cmaj7	Fmaj7
Christmas will	be a very special	

To Coda ⊕

Bm7	Em7	C#m7b5	C#7b5
Christmas	for	me.	

Interlude

D.C. al Coda

Cmaj7	G	Cmaj7	G
	3/4	4/4	

⊕ **Coda**
Outro

Repeat and fade

w/ Lead voc. ad lib.

Cmaj7	G	
	3/4	4/4

We Need a Little Christmas

from MAME

Music and Lyric by Jerry Herman

G   Dm6   E7   Am   D7   Em   G7   C

Key of G
Verse
Moderately fast

G

4/4 |: 1. Haul out the | holly. Put up the | tree be - fore my |
climb down the chimney, turn on the bright - est string of

Dm6   **E7**   **Am**   **D7**   **Am**   **D7**

| spir - it falls a - gain. | Fill up the | stocking, I may be |
lights I've ev - er seen. Slice up the fruitcake. It's time we

Am   **D7**   **Dm6**   **E7**   **Am**   **E7**

| rush - ing things, but | deck the halls a - gain | now. | 1. For we |
hung some tin - sel on the ev - er - green bough. 2. For I've

𝄋 Chorus

Am   **D7**   **G**   **Em**   **Am**   **D7**

| need a little Christmas, | right this very minute, | can - dles in the window, |
grown a little leaner, grown a little colder, grown a little sadder,
(3.) need a little music, need a little laughter, need a little singing

To Coda 🌐

G   **G7**   **C**   **D7**   **G**   **Em**

| car - ols at the spinet. Yes, we | need a little Christmas, | right this very minute. It |
grown a lit - tle older. And I need a little angel sit - ting on my shoulder. We
ring - ing through the rafter. And we need a little snappy "hap - py ever after." We

1.

A7   **D7**

| hasn't snowed a single flurry, but | Santa, dear, we're in a hurry. 2.So :||

2.

D.S. al Coda

Am   **D7**   **G**   **Am**   **E7**

| need a little Christmas | now! | 2/4 3. For we 4/4 ||

🌐 Coda

Am   **D7**   **G**

| need a little Christmas | now! ||

What Are You Doing New Year's Eve?

By Frank Loesser

C   Am7   Dm7   G7   C7   F   Fm6   D7   B7   Em   Em7   F7

Key of C
Verse
Moderately slow (♩♩ = ♩♪)

C	Am7	Dm7	G7	C	C7

4/4 Maybe   it's   much too | ear - ly   in   the game | ah, but   I thought I'd
Wonder   whose arms will | hold you good and tight | when it's   ex - act - ly

F	Fm6	C	Am7	D7

ask   you   just   the same: | What   are   you   do - ing | New   Year's,
twelve   o' - clock   that night, | wel - com - ing   in   the | new   year,

1.

G7	C

New   Year's | Eve?

2.

G7	C	B7

New   Year's | Eve.

Bridge

Em	Em7	Am7	F7	Em	Em7

Maybe   I'm crazy | to   suppose | I'd   ever   be   the

Am7	F7	Em	Em7	Am7	F7

one   you   chose | out   of   the   thousand | invitations

Outro-Verse

D7	G7	C	Am7

you'll   re - | ceive. | Ah,   but   in   case   I

Dm7	G7	C	C7	F	Fm6

stand   one   little   chance, | here comes the jackpot | question   in advance:

C	Am7	D7	G7	C

What   are   you   doing | New   Year's, | New   Year's | Eve?

White Christmas

from the Motion Picture Irving Berlin's HOLIDAY INN
Words and Music by Irving Berlin

C   Dm7   G7   Cmaj7   C7   F   Fm6   A7

Key of C
Verse
  Moderately slow

C		Dm7	G7
4/4 ‖: 1., 2. I'm	dreaming of a	white	Christmas,

Dm7	G7	Cmaj7	Dm7 G7
just like the	ones I used to	know,	where the

C Cmaj7	C7	F	Fm6
tree - tops	glisten and	children	listen to

C	Dm7	G7	
hear	sleigh bells in the	snow.	

C	Dm7	G7	
I'm	dreaming of a	white	Christmas,

Dm7	G7	Cmaj7	Dm7 G7
with ev'ry	Christmas card I	write:	"May your

C Cmaj7	C7	F	Fm6
days be	merry and	bright	and may

1.   2.

C A7	Dm7 G7	C	Dm7 G7	
all your	Christmas - es be	white."	:‖	‖

Winter Wonderland

Words by Dick Smith
Music by Felix Bernard

C   G7   D7   E   A   G   A7

Key of C

Verse
Moderately

C

| 4/4 1. Sleigh bells | : (4.) ring, | are you | list'nin'? | In the | lane, | snow is |

G7

| glist'nin'. | A | beautiful sight, | we're | happy tonight | walkin' in a winter wonder - |

D7   G7

Verse

C   **C**   **G7**

| land. | 2., 5. Gone a - | way | is the | bluebird. | Here to | stay | is a |

| new bird. | He | sings a love song | as | we go along | walkin' in a winter wonder - |

D7   G7

Bridge

C   **E**   **A**   **E**

| land. | | In the | meadow, we can build a | snowman | |

A   **E**   **G**   **C**

| { and pretend that he is Parson | Brown. | He'll say, "Are you mar - ried?" We'll say,
| { and pretend that he's a circus | clown. | We'll have lots of fun with mis - ter |

G   **A7**   **D7**   **G**

| "No, man! | But | you can do the | job when you're in | town!" } 3., 6. Later
| snow - man | un - | til the oth - er | kid - dies knock him | down! }

Verse

C   **G7**

| on | we'll con - | spire, | as we | dream | by the | fire, | to |

D7   G7

| face unafraid | the | plans that we've made | walkin' in a winter wonder - |

1.   **2.**

C   **C**

| land. | 4. Sleigh bells : | land. | |

Wonderful Christmastime

Words and Music by Paul McCartney

G   Gmaj7   Am7   D7   Bm7   Em   C   F

Key of G
Verse
Moderately

G .... **Gmaj7** .... **G** .... the ..... **G** **Gmaj7**
1. The mood is right, ... the spir - it's up, ... we're here to - night
2. The par - ty's on, ... the feel - ing's here .... that on - ly comes
3. The word is out .... a - bout the town, ... to lift a glass,

G
and that's e - nough.
this time of year.
oh, don't look down.

Chorus
Am7   D7   Bm7   Em .... **C** .... **F** ..... **G**
Sim - ply hav - ing a | wonderful Christmas - time.

Am7   D7   Bm7   Em .... **1.** **C** .... **F** ..... **G**
Sim - ply hav - ing a | wonderful Christmas - time.

2. **C** .... **F**
$\frac{2}{4}$ wonderful Christmas - $\frac{4}{4}$

Bridge
G .... **Em** .... **Am7** .... **D7** .... **G**
$\frac{4}{4}$ time. .... The | choir of children | sing their song. (They

To Coda ⊕

Em   Am7   D7   G
practiced all year | long.) .... Ding, | dong, ding, dong, ding, | dong, ding. .... We're

D.C. al Coda
(take 2nd ending)

Am7 D7 Bm7 Em ..... **C** ... **F** .... **G** .... **Am7 D7 Bm7 Em** ..... **C** ... **F** .... **G**
sim - ply hav - ing a | wonderful Christmas - time. | Sim - ply hav - ing a | wonderful Christmas - time.

⊕ **Coda**

dong, ding, dong, ding, | dong, ding, dong, ding, | dong, ding, dong, ding,

D7

Outro
G .... **Gmaj7** ... **G** ...... **Gmaj7** ... **G** .... **Gmaj7** .. **G**
dong. The party's on, | the spirit's up, | we're here tonight | and that's enough.

Repeat and fade

Am7 D7 Bm7 Em .... **C** ... **F** .... **G** .... **Am7 D7 Bm7 Em** ... **C** ... **F** .... **G**
Sim - ply hav - ing a | wonderful Christmas - time. We're | sim - ply hav - ing a | wonderful Christmas - time.

You're All I Want for Christmas

Words and Music by Glen Moore and Seger Ellis

C   G7   Dm   A7   E7   Am   D7

Key of C

Moderately slow

Verse

	C		G7	
4/4 1. You're	: all	I	want	for
	: all	I	want	for

Dm		G7			Dm	
Christmas,			all	I	want	my
Christmas,			and	if	all	my

G7		C		A7	
whole	life	through.			Each
dreams	come	true,			then

1.

Dm		E7		Am		
day	is	just	like	Christmas,		any
I'll	a -	wake	on			

D7		G7			
time	that	I'm	with	you.	2. You're

2.

C	E7		Am		
Christmas			morning	and	find

D7		G7		C	
my	stocking	filled	with	you.

Copyright © 1948 SONGS OF UNIVERSAL, INC.
Copyright Renewed
All Rights Reserved   Used by Permission

62

Celebrate Christmas
WITH YOUR GUITAR AND HAL LEONARD

THE BEST CHRISTMAS GUITAR FAKE BOOK EVER
INCLUDES TAB

Over 150 Christmas classics for guitar. Songs include: Blue Christmas • The Chipmunk Song • Frosty the Snow Man • Happy Holiday • A Holly Jolly Christmas • I Saw Mommy Kissing Santa Claus • I Wonder As I Wander • Jingle-Bell Rock • Rudolph, the Red-Nosed Reindeer • Santa Bring My Baby Back (To Me) • Suzy Snowflake • Tennessee Christmas • and more.
00240053 Melody/Lyrics/Chords..........$25.00

THE BIG CHRISTMAS COLLECTION FOR EASY GUITAR

Includes over 70 Christmas favorites, such as: Ave Maria • Blue Christmas • Deck the Hall • Feliz Navidad • Frosty the Snow Man • Happy Holiday • A Holly Jolly Christmas • Joy to the World • O Holy Night • Silver and Gold • Suzy Snowflake • and more. Does not include TAB.
00698978 Easy Guitar $17.99

CHRISTMAS CAROLS
For Easy Guitar

24 holiday favorites, including: Carol of the Bells • Good King Wenceslas • Hark! the Herald Angels Sing • I Saw Three Ships • Jingle Bells • Jolly Old St. Nicholas • O Come, O Come Immanuel • O Little Town of Bethlehem • Up on the Housetop • and more. Does not include TAB.
00702221 Easy Guitar $10.99

CHRISTMAS CAROLS
Guitar Chord Songbook

80 favorite carols for guitarists who just need the lyrics and chords: Angels We Have Heard on High • Away in a Manger • Deck the Hall • Good King Wenceslas • The Holly and the Ivy • Irish Carol • Jingle Bells • Joy to the World • O Holy Night • Rocking • Silent Night • Up on the Housetop • Welsh Carol • What Child Is This? • and more.
00699536 Lyrics/Chord Symbols/
          Guitar Chord Diagrams $14.99

CLASSICAL GUITAR CHRISTMAS SHEET MUSIC

30 top holiday songs: Away in a Manger • Deck the Hall • Go, Tell It on the Mountain • Hallelujah Chorus • I Saw Three Ships • Jingle Bells • O Little Town of Bethlehem • Silent Night • The Twelve Days of Christmas • Up on the Housetop • We Wish You a Merry Christmas • What Child Is This? • and more. Does not include TAB.
00146974 Solo Classical Guitar.............$10.99

CHRISTMAS JAZZ
INCLUDES TAB
Jazz Guitar Chord Melody Solos

21 songs in chord-melody style for the beginning to intermediate jazz guitarist in standard notation and tablature: Auld Lang Syne • Baby, It's Cold Outside • Cool Yule • Have Yourself a Merry Little Christmas • Mary, Did You Know? • Santa Baby • White Christmas • Winter Wonderland • and more.
00171334 Solo Guitar..........................$15.99

CHRISTMAS SONGS FOR EASY GUITAR

20 classic Christmas tunes: Blue Christmas • The Christmas Song (Chestnuts Roasting) • Frosty the Snow Man • Christmas Time Is Here • A Holly Jolly Christmas • I Saw Mommy Kissing Santa Claus • I'll Be Home for Christmas • Jingle-Bell Rock • Merry Christmas, Darling • Rudolph the Red-Nosed Reindeer • Silver Bells • You're All I Want for Christmas • and more.
00699804 Easy Guitar $7.99

FINGERPICKING CHRISTMAS SONGS
INCLUDES TAB

15 songs for intermediate-level guitarists, combining melody and harmony in superb fingerpicking arrangements: Baby, It's Cold Outside • Caroling, Caroling • Have Yourself a Merry Little Christmas • I Heard the Bells on Christmas Day • The Little Drummer Boy • Mary, Did You Know? • Mele Kalikimaka • Sleigh Ride • White Christmas • Wonderful Christmastime • and more.
00171333 Fingerstyle Guitar $10.99

FINGERPICKING YULETIDE
INCLUDES TAB

Carefully written for intermediate-level guitarists, this collection includes an introduction to fingerstyle guitar and 16 holiday favorites: Do You Hear What I Hear • Happy Xmas (War Is Over) • A Holly Jolly Christmas • Jingle-Bell Rock • Rudolph the Red-Nosed Reindeer • and more.
00699654 Fingerstyle Guitar $12.99

FIRST 50 CHRISTMAS CAROLS YOU SHOULD PLAY ON GUITAR
INCLUDES TAB

Accessible, must-know Christmas songs are included in this collection arranged for guitar solo with a combo of tab, chords and lyrics. Includes: Angels We Have Heard on High • The First Noel • God Rest Ye Merry, Gentlemen • The Holly and the Ivy • O Christmas Tree • Silent Night • Up on the Housetop • What Child Is This? • and more.
00236224 Guitar Solo..........................$12.99

3-CHORD CHRISTMAS

You only need to know how to play 3 chords (G, C and D) on guitar to master these 25 holiday favorites: Away in a Manger • The Chipmunk Song • Frosty the Snow Man • Go, Tell It on the Mountain • Here Comes Santa Claus • Jingle Bells • The Little Drummer Boy • O Christmas Tree • Silent Night • Silver Bells • While Shepherds Watched Their Flocks • and more.
00146973 Guitar Solo..........................$10.99

THE ULTIMATE GUITAR CHRISTMAS FAKE BOOK
INCLUDES TAB

200 Christmas standards: All I Want for Christmas Is You • Baby, It's Cold Outside • The Christmas Song (Chestnuts Roasting on an Open Fire) • Do You Want to Build a Snowman? • Feliz Navidad • Frosty the Snow Man • A Holly Jolly Christmas • Jingle Bells • Let It Snow! Let It Snow! Let It Snow! • Mary, Did You Know? • Rockin' Around the Christmas Tree • Santa Baby • Silent Night • What Child Is This? • White Christmas • and more.
00236446 Melody/Lyrics/Chords $22.50

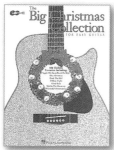

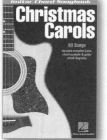

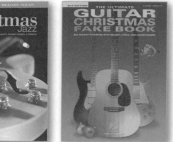

HAL•LEONARD®
www.halleonard.com

Guitar Chord Songbooks

Each 6" x 9" book includes complete lyrics, chord symbols, and guitar chord diagrams.

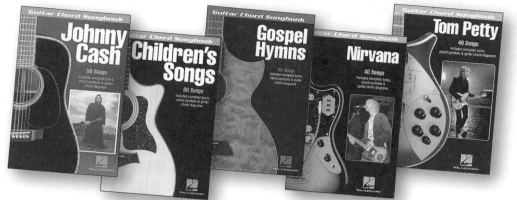

Acoustic Hits
00701787 . . . . $14.99

Acoustic Rock
00699540 . . . . $21.99

Alabama
00699914 . . . . $14.95

The Beach Boys
00699566 . . . . $19.99

The Beatles
00699562 . . . . $17.99

Bluegrass
00702585 . . . . $14.99

Johnny Cash
00699648 . . . . $17.99

Children's Songs
00699539 . . . . $16.99

Christmas Carols
00699536 . . . . $12.99

Christmas Songs
00119911 . . . . $14.99

Eric Clapton
00699567 . . . . $19.99

Classic Rock
00699598 . . . . $18.99

Coffeehouse Hits
00703318 . . . . $14.99

Country
00699534 . . . . $17.99

Country Favorites
00700609 . . . . $14.99

Country Hits
00140859 . . . . $14.99

Country Standards
00700608 . . . . $12.95

Cowboy Songs
00699636 . . . . $19.99

Creedence Clearwater Revival
00701786 . . . . $16.99

Jim Croce
00148087 . . . . $14.99

Crosby, Stills & Nash
00701609 . . . . $16.99

John Denver
02501697 . . . . $17.99

Neil Diamond
00700606 . . . . $19.99

Disney – 2nd Edition
00295786 . . . . $17.99

The Doors
00699888 . . . . $17.99

Eagles
00122917 . . . . $17.99

Early Rock
00699916 . . . . $14.99

Folksongs
00699541 . . . . $14.99

Folk Pop Rock
00699651 . . . . $17.99

40 Easy Strumming Songs
00115972 . . . . $16.99

Four Chord Songs
00701611 . . . . $14.99

Glee
00702501 . . . . $14.99

Gospel Hymns
00700463 . . . . $14.99

Grand Ole Opry®
00699885 . . . . $16.95

Grateful Dead
00139461 . . . . $14.99

Green Day
00103074 . . . . $14.99

Irish Songs
00701044 . . . . $14.99

Michael Jackson
00137847 . . . . $14.99

Billy Joel
00699632 . . . . $19.99

Elton John
00699732 . . . . $15.99

Ray LaMontagne
00130337 . . . . $12.99

Latin Songs
00700973 . . . . $14.99

Love Songs
00701043 . . . . $14.99

Bob Marley
00701704 . . . . $17.99

Bruno Mars
00125332 . . . . $12.99

Paul McCartney
00385035 . . . . $16.95

Steve Miller
00701146 . . . . $12.99

Modern Worship
00701801 . . . . $16.99

Motown
00699734 . . . . $17.99

Willie Nelson
00148273 . . . . $17.99

Nirvana
00699762 . . . . $16.99

Roy Orbison
00699752 . . . . $17.99

Peter, Paul & Mary
00103013 . . . . $19.99

Tom Petty
00699883 . . . . $15.99

Pink Floyd
00139116 . . . . $14.99

Pop/Rock
00699538 . . . . $16.99

Praise & Worship
00699634 . . . . $14.99

Elvis Presley
00699633 . . . . $17.99

Queen
00702395 . . . . $14.99

Red Hot Chili Peppers
00699710 . . . . $19.99

The Rolling Stones
00137716 . . . . $17.99

Bob Seger
00701147 . . . . $12.99

Carly Simon
00121011 . . . . $14.99

Sting
00699921 . . . . $17.99

Taylor Swift
00263755 . . . . $16.99

Three Chord Acoustic Songs
00123860 . . . . $14.99

Three Chord Songs
00699720 . . . . $17.99

Two-Chord Songs
00119236 . . . . $16.99

U2
00137744 . . . . $14.99

Hank Williams
00700607 . . . . $16.99

Stevie Wonder
00120862 . . . . $14.99

Prices and availability subject to change without notice.

Visit Hal Leonard online at **www.halleonard.com**

1120
9/12; 480